The Brave Little Turtle

written and illustrated
by Gill McBarnet

for Tara Lee

Also published by Ruwanga Trading:
The Whale Who Wanted to be Small
The Wonderful Journey
A Whale's Tale
The Shark Who Learned a Lesson
The Goodnight Gecko
Gecko Hide and Seek
The Gift of Aloha
Tikki Turtle's Quest

First published 1994 by Ruwanga Trading
ISBN 0-9615102-8-5
Printed in China through Everbest Printing Co., Ltd.
BOOK ENQUIRIES:
Booklines Hawaii Ltd.
269 Pali'i Street
Mililani, Hawaii. 96789
Phone: (808) 676-0116
E-mail: bookline@lava.net

This is a story about a brave little turtle called Nani, who lives in the sparkling blue ocean around the Hawaiian islands. Nani was not always brave. In fact, she used to be very timid, until something happened that made her the bravest turtle EVER.

But let's begin at the beginning…

O

ne day, not so very long ago, Nani the turtle hatched out of her egg.

Her egg was one of many that her mother had buried in the soft warm sand. She peeped shyly out, and was pushed aside by the other little turtles as they scrambled out of the nest. One of them stood near her, stretching his tiny flippers and snapping his little beak. "What are you waiting for?" he chirped. "Come on, I'll race you to the ocean!"

From that moment on, Nani and Lono were best friends.

Nani was as timid and careful as Lono was bold and carefree. His boldness helped them as they scrambled down to the ocean. Big birds tried to pick them up with their sharp black beaks. Nani froze in terror, but Lono called to her to follow him.

Together, they dodged the sharp beaks and claws, by hiding under bits of seaweed, stones or chunks of coral. Safe at last, they made it into the waves that washed the beach. Flicking their little flippers, Nani and Lono were soon speeding away through the warm blue ocean.

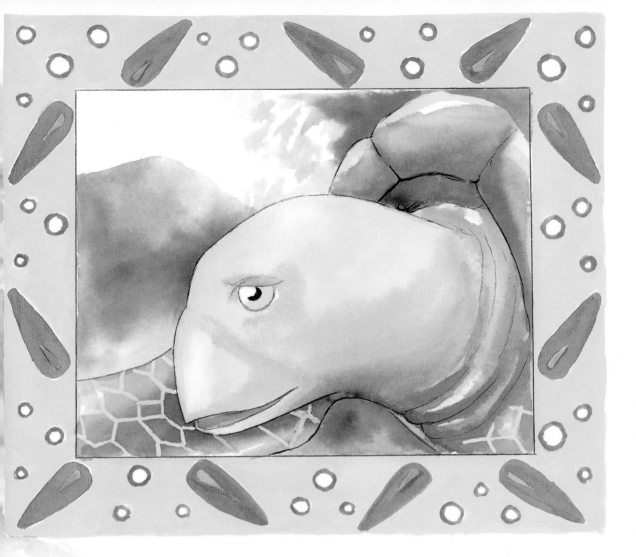

Time went by, and the ocean was a playground for the two turtles. Lono was a show-off. He tried to get Nani to do the bold things that he loved doing... like catching the biggest waves that thundered and crashed as they broke.

"Look at me. Surf with me, Nani!" he would shout. "But those waves look so big and scary. What if my shell is smashed into a thousand pieces?" Nani would reply from gently rolling waves.

"Lono has so much fun. How I wish I were bold like him, but I'm always so timid and careful," Nani would sigh.

"Let's explore this cave, Nani!" Lono would say. "Maybe we'll find some treasure hidden in the shadows."

"Those shadows make me shiver. I'd love to find treasure, Lono, but what if we only find sharks?" Nani would reply, trying not to tremble at the thought of hungry sharks hiding in the shadows.

"How I wish I were brave, but I get so scared." Nani would sigh.

Lono was such a dare-devil. Sometimes he would dive down into the deep, dark ocean, where only strange looking creatures live. He would go with Kona the baby sperm whale, and would call back to Nani to join them. "How I wish I were brave enough to follow you, but it looks so dark and cold down there. What if it becomes so dark that I cannot see? And what if I run out of air?" Nani would say.

Lono loved excitement. He never stopped to think about danger, and he always teased Nani about being so careful.

And so it was, one sunny day, the two turtles saw a red boat not far from where they were playing. Lono immediately wanted to get a closer look. "Stay away!" said Nani. "Don't you remember Grandpa turtle's warning? Boats carry humans, and humans bring danger to turtles…"
"Oh Nani. You're scared of everything!" said Lono. "If you're not brave enough to come with me, I'll go alone…" And with that, he swam up to the boat.

The humans were throwing trash into the ocean. Always curious, Lono swam through what he thought was a strange new type of seaweed. He glided gleefully through the discarded fishing line, net and other plastic trash, and when he surfaced some of the trash hung like an untidy necklace around his neck.
"What is that?" called Nani. "Come here so I can bite it off." "It's nothing to fuss about," laughed Lono. "By tomorrow it will have fallen off."

But tomorrow came and went, and the plastic necklace did not fall off. The next day and the day after that came and went… but still the necklace did not fall off. By now, Lono's neck was beginning to swell, and the necklace was becoming tight and uncomfortable on his neck. Nani tried to bite it off with her sharp beak, but the plastic was so strong, she wasn't even able to make a tiny dent in it.

"Here! I'll pull it off easily with my strong arms," said Tako the octopus confidently. But no matter how much he pulled and pulled with all eight powerful arms, the octopus was not able to remove the necklace.

A passing group of Butterfly fish asked if they could help. "Don't worry, Lono. We'll each take it in turn to nibble away at the necklace, and in no time you'll be free again!" They were joined by the Rainbow Wrasse family, the bold Humu Humu and Pikaki the parrot fish.

But although all the fish nibbled and nibbled for a very long time, none of them was able to remove the necklace.

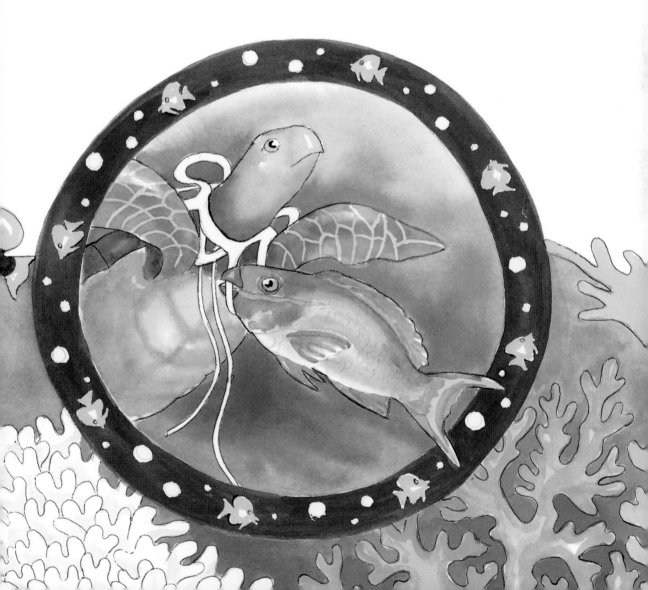

The necklace got tighter and tighter. It was becoming difficult for Lono to breath properly or swallow his food, so he became weaker and weaker. Nani did everything she could to help Lono.

She asked Hoku the swordfish to break the necklace off Lono's neck. But no matter how hard Hoku tried to snap it off, the plastic necklace was much too strong even for Hoku's powerful sword!

Leilani the sea anemone and her sisters offered to help. "We will use the strong juices we use to break down our food, to break the necklace," Leilani said. The anemones wrapped their tiny tentacles around the necklace and squirted it with their strong juices, but the juices were not powerful enough to break the necklace.

Kaleela the eel with his strong jaws, also tried to help. Lastly, even Peeko the crab tried to remove the necklace with his sharp claws… but none of the sea creatures were able to break the necklace.

Tears trickled down Lono's cheeks. "It's no use, Nani. I'll never get it off my neck, and now I'm so weak I can hardly swim to the surface for air." "Don't give up, Lono!" said Nani with sudden boldness. "I'll find a way to help you… you'll see!" And with that she pushed Lono to the surface of the ocean, so he could fill his lungs with air.

The quiet voice of Dano the dolphin spoke up. "The necklace is too strong for us to break, Nani. Many of our brothers and sisters have swallowed or become tangled up in this terrible weed that the humans throw into our ocean."

"But there must be a way to take it off his neck!" cried Nani. "I'm afraid the only creatures with the power to break it... are the ones who hurt us with it in the first place. Humans!" Dano replied.

"Then that is what I must do. I must take Lono to some good humans, and hope that they will help him." said Nani. "I have seen small humans playing on Golden Beach, so that is where we must go."

"No, no. I don't want to go!" said Lono in a feeble and frightened voice. "The humans have already hurt me. I don't want them to hurt me even more!"
"It's a risk we must take, Lono, because although it is their trash that is hurting you, they are the only ones with the power to free you of it. " said Nani.
"Don't go, Nani! You might also get hurt!" cried all the other sea creatures.

"I am scared to go but I must, if I want to save Lono... " Nani replied. "How would you like it if you needed help, and no one wanted to help YOU?"
The sea creatures nodded quietly, as Nani started pushing Lono towards Golden Beach.

The waves were high and crashing over her head, but Nani pushed Lono through the pounding surf. Her muscles were sore from all the pushing when suddenly ahead of her... Golden Beach glowed in the sunshine!

Gently she pushed Lono onto the sand and, looking up, she saw two little humans walking towards them. Her heart fluttered nervously, but she forced herself to stay with Lono. The little humans then stopped abruptly, and raced away. They soon returned with a big human. Instinct made her want to turn and flee, back to the safety of the sea. It was all she could do, to force herself to stay on the beach, but Nani knew that she had to be brave, to save Lono.

Unexpectedly, a strange feeling filled her body. She felt strong and confident like never before, and she sensed that these humans were here as friends. Lono was trembling all over. He was terrified, so Nani gave him a comforting pat with her flipper.

The humans were quiet and gentle, and the big human sat next to them in the sand and gently stroked Lono's shell. "Poor thing. Look what he has around his neck! No wonder he is so weak." It felt soothing to be touched so gently. "This is what happens when we throw our trash into the ocean. We are hurting our friends, the sea creatures!" said the big human angrily.

The little humans were sad and ashamed to think that such carelessness is hurting many sea creatures. "Can we save the turtle?" asked the one little human. "Yes, I think he will be strong enough to survive, but first I must take this off his neck." A flash of silver. Snip, snip… and the big human gently took the plastic necklace off Lono's neck.

Lono took a deep breath, and immediately felt better.

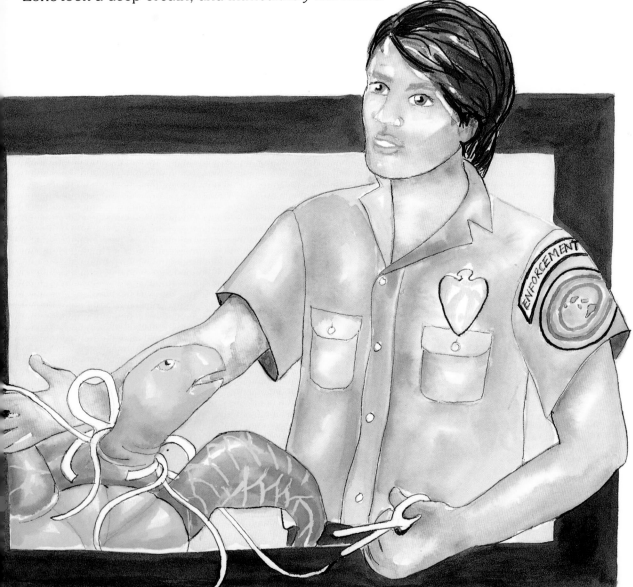

Nani didn't understand what the humans were saying, but she liked their voices, and she was so happy that they had helped Lono. Her eyes shone with gratitude as she looked up at the big human.

The big human stroked Nani's shell, and he said with a smile. "And you, Brave One… are you here to protect your friend? Come along now, children, we must leave the turtles alone so that they can recover in peace and quiet."
With that, the humans walked quietly away.

Nani and Lono lay basking in the sun, feeling the warmth fill their tired bodies with golden energy.

Lono said, "I used to think I was being brave, but I was really just showing off and taking silly risks. Bravery is getting yourself or someone else out of danger, even when you are afraid. You saved my life even though it meant you were putting yourself in danger. You are the bravest turtle EVER!"

The brave little turtle smiled. She knew now that she could be brave and strong when she needed to be, and this made her feel proud and happy. She was also hungry…

"Come on, Lono. What are you waiting for? I'll race you to the ocean!!" shouted the brave little turtle.